THE BATTLES OF LEXINGTON AND CONCORD

A DAY THAT CHANGED AMERICA

by Isaac Kerry

CAPSTONE PRESS
a capstone imprint

Published by Capstone Press, an imprint of Capstone
1710 Roe Crest Drive, North Mankato, Minnesota 56003
capstonepub.com

Library of Congress Cataloging-in-Publication Data
Names: Kerry, Isaac, author.
Title: The battles of Lexington and Concord : a day that changed America / by Isaac Kerry.
Description: North Mankato, Minnesota : Published by Capstone Press, an imprint of Capstone, [2023] | Series: Days that changed America | Includes bibliographical references and index. | Audience: Ages 8-11 | Audience: Grades 4-6 | Summary: "For years, the relationship between Great Britain and the American colonists had been wearing thin. Colonists felt they were being treated unfairly. The British thought they were putting down a rebellion. On April 19, 1775, the two sides clashed at Lexington and Concord. The American Revolution was about to begin. Now readers can step back in time to learn about what led up to the battles, how the historic events unfolded, and the ways in which one shot changed America forever"—Provided by publisher.
Identifiers: LCCN 2021061507 (print) | LCCN 2021061508 (ebook) | ISBN 9781666341560 (hardcover) | ISBN 9781666341577 (paperback) | ISBN 9781666341584 (pdf) | ISBN 9781666341607 (kindle edition)
Subjects: LCSH: Lexington, Battle of, Lexington, Mass., 1775—Juvenile literature. | Concord, Battle of, Concord, Mass., 1775—Juvenile literature. | United States—History—Revolution, 1775–1783—Juvenile literature.
Classification: LCC E241.L6 K47 2023 (print) | LCC E241.L6 (ebook) | DDC 973.3/311—dc23/eng/20211217
LC record available at https://lccn.loc.gov/2021061507
LC ebook record available at https://lccn.loc.gov/2021061508

Editorial Credits
Editor: Book Buddy Media; Media Researcher: Morgan Walters; Production Specialist: Polly Fisher

Consultant Credits
Richard Bell
Associate Professor of History
University of Maryland, College Park

Image Credits
Courtesy of the Council of the National Army Museum, London, 16; Getty Images: bauhaus1000, 13, ivan-96, 10, Keith Lance, 11; Library of Congress, 25; National Portrait Gallery, Smithsonian Institution, 12; National Postal Museum, 7; Red Line Editorial, 5; Shutterstock: Jay Yuan, 4, Alex Fleming, 20, Atoly , Christian Delbert, 22, Diego Grandi, 15, Everett Collection, 9, 21, 27, quiggyt4, 17; The New York Public Library, 19, 24; Wikimedia, 8, National Park Service, 18

Printed and bound in the USA. 4882

TABLE OF CONTENTS

Introduction 4

CHAPTER 1
Taxation Without Representation 6

CHAPTER 2
Repression and Rebellion 10

CHAPTER 3
On Lexington Green 12

CHAPTER 4
The Battle of Concord 18

CHAPTER 5
A Rebellion Begins 24

Timeline 28

Glossary 30

Read More 31

Internet Sites 31

Index 32

Words in **bold** are in the glossary.

During the 1700s, Great Britain was one of the most powerful nations in the world. British **colonies** existed all over the world. Colonists sent resources like tobacco and wood back to Britain. These colonies made England extremely wealthy. In 1607, England established its first permanent colony in North America. By 1775, there were 13 British colonies along the Atlantic coast. More than 2 million colonists and 460,000 enslaved people lived there.

For many years, the colonists had been content under British rule. However, in the 1770s, that started to change. The British government made some unpopular laws. **Protests** were spreading. The colonists of Massachusetts were especially upset. Lexington and Concord were two small towns in Massachusetts. They would be where the American Revolution began.

The Battle of Lexington is now a historic site.

New Hampshire

Massachusetts

Rhode Island

Connecticut

New York

Pennsylvania

New Jersey

Delaware

Maryland

Virginia

North Carolina

South Carolina

Georgia

ATLANTIC OCEAN

GULF OF MEXICO

N
W   E
S

Present-day U.S. map showing the 13 original British colonies in red

CHAPTER 1

TAXATION WITHOUT REPRESENTATION

The road to rebellion started in 1765. The Seven Years' War (1756–1763) had ended. Britain had fought France for control of North America. Britain won, but the war had been expensive. **Parliament** wanted the colonists to pay their share. The Stamp Act was passed. The Stamp Act required a stamp on all printed paper. Each stamp cost money.

Many colonists thought the Stamp Act was unfair. But they had no way to make their opinions heard by the British government. They did not have anyone speaking for them in Parliament. The slogan "no taxation without representation" became popular.

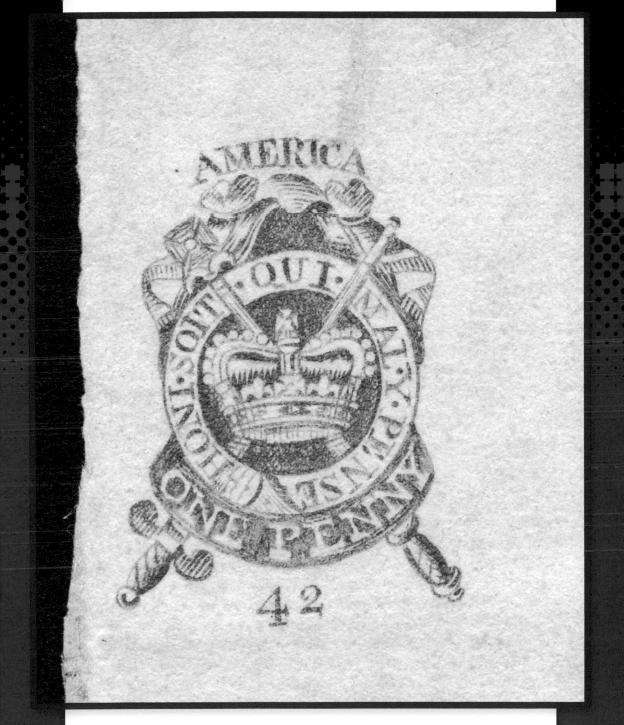

The British government passed the Stamp Act without hearing the colonists' opinion. All legal documents and printed material needed to have this stamp applied.

Protests spread throughout the colonies. Some colonists protested peacefully by writing to officials and organizing **boycotts** of British goods. Others were more violent. A group called the Sons of Liberty formed. They threatened British officials. They vandalized shops owned by people who followed British rules. Due to these protests, the Stamp Act was **repealed** in 1766. But it was too little, too late.

The Green Dragon Tavern was a meeting place for the Sons of Liberty.

By 1770, there were thousands of British troops in the city of Boston. They were there to enforce the British laws. In March, a fight broke out between the soldiers and townspeople. Five colonists were killed. This became known as the Boston Massacre. The Sons of Liberty used the massacre to spread anti-British **propaganda**.

Paul Revere's engraving was not an accurate depiction of what happened at the Boston Massacre. It was meant to anger the colonists.

FACT

The famous engraving of the Boston Massacre was created by a silversmith named Paul Revere. He would go on to play a key role in the Battles of Lexington and Concord.

CHAPTER 2

REPRESSION AND REBELLION

In 1773, Parliament passed the Tea Act. It allowed only one company to sell tea in the colonies. Many colonists were against it. Anti-British feelings kept growing. Unruly colonists continued making trouble for Britain. They raided ships in Boston Harbor. On December 16, 1773, protesters dressed in American Indian costumes threw tea into the Boston Harbor. This became known as the Boston Tea Party.

Colonists dumped 342 chests of tea into the Boston Harbor.

Now, Britain's eye was focused on Boston. In 1774, Parliament passed the Coercive Acts. These laws were to punish Massachusetts. They blocked the port of Boston. No ships could go in or out. Elections were stopped. Instead, the governor was given more power. Britain lost even more supporters. **Militias** began forming across the colony. In 1775, Parliament declared Massachusetts as a place of rebellion.

It took almost three hours to dump 90,000 pounds (40,823 kilograms) of tea into the harbor.

CHAPTER 3

ON LEXINGTON GREEN

General Thomas Gage was the military governor of Massachusetts. On April 14, 1775, he was ordered to stop the rebel militias. Gage knew that Patriots had been storing supplies. The small village of Concord was a known location. It was about 20 miles (32 kilometers) from Boston.

Gage also wanted to capture the rebel leaders Samuel Adams and John Hancock. Both men had recently fled to the town of Lexington. Lexington was on the way to Concord.

John Hancock (1737–1793) was a rich merchant. He helped raise money for the Patriots.

Samuel Adams (1722–1803) was one of the first colonists to speak out against taxation without representation.

On the night of April 18, Gage called his officers. They planned to take around 700 troops to Concord. Their goal was to capture or destroy any supplies they found. Gage tried to keep the mission secret by meeting at night. But several Patriot spies were watching. One sent word to a doctor named Joseph Warren. Warren passed his information along to Paul Revere.

Revere rode out from the city with a warning. He told people he met along the way that the British were coming. Revere warned Adams and Hancock in Lexington.

Lexington put out a call for aid. Nearly 80 militia members answered. Their commander was Captain John Parker. Parker was a veteran of the Seven Years' War. He knew his troops were outnumbered. The supplies at Concord had already been moved. He did not want to face the British. His goal was to show the militia's strength as the British marched by.

FACT

John Parker was related to about 20 of the militia soldiers assembled at Lexington.

The Paul Revere statue is one of the most recognizable locations in Boston, Massachusetts.

The shot fired at Lexington Green was called "the shot heard 'round the world."

The militia stood on the town green, waiting. The British troops came down the road. Neither side wanted a fight. A British officer rode out. He yelled at the colonists to throw down their arms. Parker ordered his troops to leave the field. However, there was confusion and yelling. A gun was fired. No one knows to whom the gun belonged.

The shot started a chain reaction. A few scattered musket shots from both sides rang out. Soon, though, the British soldiers sent organized **volleys**. Eight militiamen died. Ten were wounded. There was one British **casualty**. The British restored order to their forces. They continued their march to Concord.

A memorial to the Lexington minutemen stands across the street from where the battle was fought.

WHAT IS A "MINUTEMAN"?

Colonial militias are sometimes called "minutemen." This is only partially correct. Some of the militias in Massachusetts had a special company known as a "minute company." These men were often younger and had special training. Their goal was to get ready for battle "at a minute's notice." About one-fourth of a militia's members were part of the minute company.

CHAPTER 4

THE BATTLE OF CONCORD

After Paul Revere warned Lexington, he rode for Concord. He was captured along the way. A doctor named Samuel Prescott was able to continue on. He gave the militia plenty of time to prepare. When the British arrived, the militia was about 400 strong. Their commander was Colonel James Barrett. He, too, knew the British Army was larger. He ordered his men to retreat to a hill near the town. There, they would wait for reinforcements.

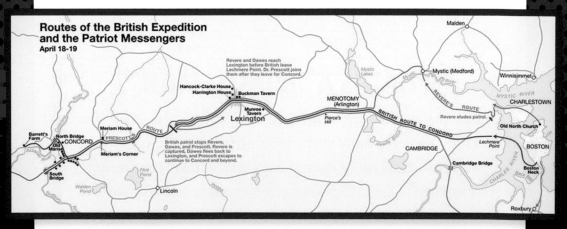

The routes from Lexington to Concord.

Paul Revere published stories about his ride. Later, poet Henry Wadsworth Longfellow wrote about it.

THE OTHER RIDERS

Paul Revere's ride is a famous part of American history. But it leaves out two other important figures. A man named William Dawes also rode out from Boston. He took a different route to Lexington than Revere. This let him alert different towns. It also meant there would be another rider if one was captured. Dawes arrived at Lexington shortly after Revere. Samuel Prescott joined them there. The three rode for Concord together. However, they were stopped by British riders. Only Prescott made it through to warn Concord.

Cannons called field guns were lightweight and easy to move.

The British began searching Concord. They found three cannons buried in the ground. They also discovered food and musket balls. The British threw the supplies into a river. They burned the cannons. But the fire grew out of control. Its flames spread to a nearby building. British troops helped the villagers put it out.

The militia saw the smoke rising from the town. They did not know the British were helping put out the fire. Barrett thought the soldiers were destroying the village. The militia marched to the North Bridge leading into Concord. Around 90 British troops met the 400 militiamen. The British were on the defense. The Patriots had strict orders not to fire unless fired upon.

The first image of the Battle of Lexington was printed in December 1775. The two militiamen who created it were not at the battle themselves.

People can still visit Concord's North Bridge today.

No order to fire was given, but one British soldier did. Like in Lexington, other soldiers began shooting as well. Several militiamen were hit and two were killed. The colonists fired back. This resulted in many casualties. After the volleys were over, both groups retreated. No further fighting happened in Concord.

Around noon, the British finished their search. They prepared to return to Boston. More militiamen had arrived, though. They attacked the British. The British troops were exhausted. They were low on ammunition. British reinforcements met them at Lexington. Several more fights took place on the journey to Boston. More and more militiamen kept arriving. By the next day, there were at least 15,000 troops. Boston was now under **siege**.

FACT

Muskets were not very accurate weapons. Most firing was done within 75 to 150 feet (23 to 46 meters) of the enemy.

A REBELLION BEGINS

At the end of the day, 49 colonists and 73 British soldiers were killed. Another 39 colonists and 174 British soldiers were wounded. The British Army was one of the finest fighting forces in the world. They had fought wars with huge countries like France and Spain. The losses at Concord showed the colonists they could be beaten.

The battles were a turning point in colonial support for independence.

In March, Parliament had drafted a new law. It was called the Conciliatory Proposition. It promised that the colonies would no longer be taxed. It was made formal on March 30, two weeks before Lexington and Concord. It took a long time for news to reach America. By the time the act arrived, the battles had already taken place. It was too late to stop the war.

Lord Frederick North was the prime minister of Great Britain during the war. Some people blamed him for not being able to stop the revolution.

Before the Battles of Lexington and Concord, many colonists were still unsure whether war was the right answer. The fighting was used to turn public opinion toward war. Even though events on the day were unclear, the blame was laid on the British. Adams and others spread the story that the British fired first and killed innocent farmers. Support for fighting back grew throughout the colonies.

In May, the Second Continental Congress met in Philadelphia. They voted to create an official colonial army. Its first members were the militia units who still surrounded the city of Boston. Soon, George Washington took command. The militia would become the Continental Army. The American Revolution had begun. Over the next eight years, the American colonists battled the British Army all throughout the colonies. Finally, in 1783, the Treaty of Paris was signed. It gave the colonies their independence and set the stage for a new nation to be born.

George Washington (front, on horse) served as America's first president from 1789 to 1797.

TIMELINE

FEBRUARY 10, 1763: The Seven Years' War ends.

MARCH 22, 1765: Parliament passes the Stamp Act.

MARCH 5, 1770: British troops shoot five Boston townspeople in an event known as the Boston Massacre.

APRIL 27, 1773: Parliament passes the Tea Act.

DECEMBER 16, 1773: Colonists raid ships in Boston Harbor and throw tea overboard. This becomes known as the Boston Tea Party.

MARCH 31–JUNE 22, 1774: Parliament passes the Coercive Acts.

APRIL 14, 1775: General Gage receives orders to capture militia supplies.

APRIL 18, 1775: Seven hundred British troops set out for Concord.

APRIL 19, 1775:

12:00 A.M.: Paul Revere arrives in Lexington. William Dawes rides in shortly after. Captain Parker assembles the militia.

2:00 A.M.: Samuel Prescott arrives in Concord.

5:30 A.M.: British soldiers arrive at Lexington. Shots are fired.

7:00 A.M.: The British arrive at Concord.

9:30 A.M.: Colonial militia clash with British troops at the North Bridge.

2:00 P.M.: The British retreat to Lexington. They find reinforcements there.

12:00 A.M.: British troops arrive back in Boston.

GLOSSARY

boycott (BOY-kot)—form of protest that involves refusing to buy goods from a business or government

casualty (KAZH-oo-uhl-tee)—a person killed, wounded, or missing in a battle or in a war

colony (KAH-luh-nee)—an area that has been settled by people from another country; a colony is ruled by another country

militia (muh-LISH-uh)—a group of volunteer citizens who serve as soldiers in emergencies

Parliament (PAR-luh-muhnt)—the group of British people who have been elected to make the laws in Great Britain

propaganda (praw-puh-GAN-duh)—information spread to try to influence the thinking of people; often not completely true or fair

protest (PRO-test)—a gathering of people to show disagreement with a law or idea

repeal (ri-PEEL)—to officially cancel something, such as a law

siege (SEEJ)—an attack designed to surround a place and cut it off from supplies or help

volley (VOL-ee)—multiple gunshots fired at the same time